ALL OF US RETICENT, HERE, TOGETHER

OTHER BOOKS BY THE AUTHOR

Where Did You See It Last? (Textualis Press, 2016)
Declassified Nuclear Test Films (above/ground press, 2014)
Complete Surprising Fragments of Improbable Books (Mansfield Press, 2013)
Excerpts from Improbable Books, The Apt. 9 Installment (Apt. 9 Press, 2013)
Excerpts from Impossible Books, The Crawdad Cantos (above/ground press, 2012)
Impossible Books, The Carleton Installment (above/ground press, 2010)
From Impossible Books (Olive Reading Series, 2007)
The Real Made Up (ECW Press, 2007)
O Helios (Olive Reading Series, 2005)
Fruitfly Geographic (ECW Press, 2004)
Cometology (ECW Press, 2001)
Marin County Poems (above/ground press, 2001)
The Wire in Fences (Balmuir Poetry Series, 1988)

ALL OF US RETICENT, HERE, TOGETHER

STEPHEN
BROCKWELL

Mansfield Press

a stuart ross book

Printed in Canada

Library and Archives Canada Cataloguing in Publication

Brockwell, Stephen, author
All of us reticent, here, together / Stephen Brockwell.

Poems.
ISBN 978-1-77126-129-6 (paperback)

I. Title.

PS8553.R6135A64 2016 C811'.54 C2016-906171-X

Editor for the Press: Stuart Ross
Typesetting & Cover Design: Stuart Ross
Author Photo: rob mclennan

The publication of *All of Us Reticent, Here, Together* has been generously supported by the Canada Council for the Arts and the Ontario Arts Council.

Canada Council for the Arts Conseil des arts du Canada

ONTARIO ARTS COUNCIL
CONSEIL DES ARTS DE L'ONTARIO
an Ontario government agency
un organisme du gouvernement de l'Ontario

Mansfield Press Inc.
25 Mansfield Avenue, Toronto, Ontario, Canada M6J 2A9
Publisher: Denis De Klerck
www.mansfieldpress.net

CONTENTS

LOST THINGS

When you found the lost thing on the side of the road
in the gravel, in the mud there, near the rainbow
of the oil slick,
you missed the things that other people found
before you found that thing
and you missed the things not yet
found that didn't catch your eye,
conditioned as your eye was to catch
a flash of light
not colour
or a blur of darkness
not light,
and there it was in your hand, a
shining or a black thing (also shining)
you could not describe to save your life,
a jewel from a lost ring or
a fragment of a loop from a mother's earring or
the mother of pearl from a brooch
cracked and detached from its metal by a rolling tire
or maybe it was a tar-encrusted glass marble
dropped from a paving truck—you seem to recall it was—
it was the first thing you knew you had found
giving *find* its meaning
and you lost it, and the memory of it, you moron!

THE LOCATION OF CULTURE

At a truckstop counter in Paris.

Over by the Starbucks in Nagoya, I didn't understand a word. Inside Zanzibar's Coffee Adventure, finest beans in Iowa, I caught a word I knew.

Curbside near a Philly cheesesteak joint on a sizzling Friday in August, Brandon insists we take it with Cheez Whiz.

Under plane trees and palms at the San Diego Zoo, polar bears soak on wet concrete.

Underneath the oak, a bench has been installed, site for lapdogs, evening weed, Viola-Cesario soliloquies.

Through the ear canal, the caw of the crow on the street lamp resonates in the ossicles.

Across Coltrane's reed.

In deer-hide drums I wish I had an ear for.

In neck, fret, and peg, braced spruce and manicured nail. Through humbucker and valve.

At the Blackburn Arms where Jack McGuire performs songs no one hears over the off-key accompaniment of hammered regulars.

Through noise-cancelling Beats, Bluetooth Queen of the Night.

Notwithstanding my mother's Sinatra, my daughter's #queenbey.

Throughout the exhausted sleeper's veins. Between treatment and injection site. In small-print contraindications.

In bed, in a hammock between trees, in the bath, on moss, in cold lakes, our bodies pair by prepositions.

On the lips of the toddler smooshing pages with jam. In the theatre of her hands. She tilts her head to the right, mimics her father's imitative coos.

Throughout the primary school hallways when the bell rings on a May scorcher as the shrieks of recessing kids are at their peak.

At the public library beside the canal, on a table behind rare-book stacks, volumes open, spread.

Between the pages of my great-uncle Eddie's *Leaves of Grass*. In the handshake of his Bajan lover, Colin.

On the handles of my grandfather's paintbrushes: accidental abstract expressionism.

In the cellar, inside the chest with mould-dusted leather locking straps: "Man on the Moon" newspapers, a loaded handgun, plastic-wrapped vintage pornography, rags sharp with turpentine.

Inside shelves installed in his dresser drawers, we found the alphabetized complete works of Edgar Rice Burroughs, Louis L'Amour and Zane Grey.

Toward Mont Royal's cross, the white spruce, or the fly on the window at the Montreal General Hospital where my father's eyes finally settled.

In Parc Jarry bleachers, hot dog in mouth as Bailey singles Woods home. In the T-shirt's cherished mustard stain.

In Muzak accompanying the Zamboni's peculiar figures.

At Aréna Robert Guertin, in locker rooms of broken sticks, what might Guy Lafleur's poster eyes have seen?

On the court, hoops; in court, hoops.

Around the ditch where the sewer crew shovels through effluent, hoping to find and close a valve.

Abaft the engine room, reeking of fish and fuel.

From the combine harvester's thousand-watt stereo, barley field Marley.

Under the boardroom table of the princes of power, bless their blue silk ties, there's gum. For all their financial instruments, pick your prepositions; govern them by sharp verbs.

In my mother's blueprints for Montreal trunks.

Over the copper pair, the glass fibre, between towers:
packets of everything. We like it.

Under the Cisco bridge, trolls creep.

In diodes emitting a radiant moving window of briefest
eternity.

In the palimpsest of typewriter roller and plasma screen,
PINs for accounts of the poorest and richest.

In Homer.

Between rings in birch grain, inside axe and saw cuts,
under initialled bark.

Under the throat of the slaughtered calf, along the blade of
the sakin.

At the cathedral for her funeral, in liturgy and hymn,
unexpected comfort.

In the LAV—none of us wants to hear it—when the RPG
renders acronyms disgusting.

@Cranium Central Station, a bat in the attic hangs itself
to sleep.

TONGUE LASHING

Of course every word has a root.
And you have a spade
and loam to grow it,
soiled.

A spider diagram of tongues
adheres a word to a web
of lore, fixing it there to
feast on its saliva-diluted blood.

A tarsal history of the foot of the word
steps out of the ancestral sole,
wide, callused, into a flip-flop-
bedded, pedicured beach foot.

Imagine borrowing the word,
signing a promissory note:
a pledge you pray
you can pay back.

You witnessed a miraculous
conjunction of the eyes and cheekbones.
It impressed your retina
with reflected lumens, leaving
your breath stopped, insisting
on a word new
to the ear and tongue,
from *ur-sprache* early in the alphabet,
from the Cratalytic converter,
a slanted Czech movie word,
subtitle for an apt transcription
of the heart's translation
of the eye's exuberant feast.

Find the word that hurdles
onto the pink springboard
of the tongue, pikes,
plies the air, rips its entry
into the waiting dictionaries
of improvised speech, prior to
the page, inked in the ear,
linked in its companion
cerebral circuits, burned-in,
encaustic, a word that schleps
from the tongue, all root,
no plant, all rhizome, no bud.

When you make Procrustes a bed,
forge telescoping brass tubes
to lay the frame. He'll fit.
From 4' to 7' he'll fit
as easily as anyone with a ponytail
unwraps the Gordian knot
with one hand, without sight
or a sword.

Say, "Bigger needle,
smaller camel." Bankers
will dance at your table with
mortgages secured only by
words you have yet to think of
or mutter in your sleep.

BIOGRAPHY OF THE TRANSLUCENT GRANDMOTHER

I can't remember my grandmother's face
with youthful skin though she would have been
early forties when I was born. Her skin
was a lampshade stretched over her body;
the posts of her frame supported—not like bamboo

but like the one-season stalks of wild
Scottish thistles—a skull with eyes that had burned out.
Doris was an antique child from the moment
she married my grandfather who taught her
the acrobatic art of tumbling

intoxicated down the kitchen hallway.
As soon as my mother learned to smoke
she tried to raise Doris as one of her own
but buried the thought of Doris's nylons,
blood-tinted at the knees.

REPLY TO CRUEL WORDS FROM DR. SCHOTT

Hold on, you're telling me to think about
acts of cruelty others have endured?
Find me a man who hasn't been cruel,
punched nobody in the face at lunch
under the tetherball, waited for no one
to walk home so he could jump from the bushes
and test his back-breaker, never slut-shamed
Susan for sticking her tongue out in math,
tripped no kid on the skating rink at recess
making nobody puke from a concussion,
never called Albert a homo for crossing swords,
didn't pretend to film Maddog Hotdog
freaking out after his weekly wedgie,
never shot a sparrow off a fence post.
Didn't too forcefully kiss a reluctant dance partner.
Didn't lock a kid in their room for cursing.
Refused to slash the tires of the shithead
who forced you and your mother off the road.
Never made his patients feel worthless.
Never pulled the forelegs off a horsefly.
Maybe this was too specific. What's that?
I should line them all up in my mind's eye,
apologize to each and ask forgiveness?
On this calm November evening,
anniversary of my mother's death,
under a full moon veiled like a bride—
or, as I imagine a bride to be—
by cirrostratus clouds that let a handful
of the brightest stars glimmer through pinholes
in the sky, we're looking at one long queue
of sad shadows soon to be disappointed.

REFLECTIONS ON A PERCEIVED MOMENT OF SOLITUDE

Woke after an all-nighter.
Who hasn't? Night ends
when we lose consciousness
of it: at 2, 3, or 4
someone is going under
as another opens an eyelid
to deliver newspapers,
packages, patients. So—
woke. Silent street. Not a dog.
No tree breeze. Squirrels asleep.
Diffuse sunlight. Enough
to see the boundary between
the sidewalk and the grass,
to cast a shadow from an oak.
No cats. Silent dog. No kids.
The impression of my wife's body
on the mattress. No coffee. No bacon.
That leaf has different shades of green
on the top, where light reflects,
and underneath, where the oak
exchanges air. Yearning.
The world's exhausted.
I meant the word—the word
yearn is zonked. So many years
of it, widely dispersed. Never
have I been so happy to receive
a smart phone's Mozart ring-tone
ping, an alert bearing
a tweet with tragic news.

INAPPROPRIATE EULOGY FOR FRED SIMS

He was awkward among his peers
in the way a baby squab is awkward
in a puddle in the street below the nest,
as a pastor is ungainly after New Year's Eve
beers, the first after many dry years,
as the fifteen-year-old lad is tentative
when castrating his first steer
(his impatient father scowling),
as the adolescent girl is discomfited
by her great uncle's undisguised leers,
as the Africadian defenceman is shamed
by the home crowd's racist jeers
(were some of us not seated with the crowd?),
as you, Fred, trembled with regret
when I told your wife about Francine,
as all of us are reticent, here, together.
A practiced smile could not replace
the guileless grace you had, once,
Fred, before your poems and your ex-wife
fell upon you like that PWN1 virus.

BIOGRAPHY OF GLAZING

Pain his reserved word for behaviour management:
"There will be pain if you keep that up!"
But I don't recall him tanning my hide.
He was more of a painter, carpenter,
and part-time glazier, a safe bet for a former
rookie cop who shot himself in the foot
in hot pursuit of a thief on Greene Avenue.
When he toppled under the living room
picture window he had pulled out to glaze,
I observed, baffled, the small hand of my
grandfather's body rotate from noon to three.
Let my grandson never rifle through my drawers
to find my nitroglycerin prescription
and race it to me, three concrete steps at a stride.

DRIVING IN THE COUNTRY IS BLOODY MURDER

I'm driving up to a murder
and realize I've never seen
a crow hit by a car.
Does that mean I've witnessed
evolution in my lifetime,
that all the crows that might have been
whacked by tires or windshields
were whacked between, let's say,
the '50s and the '70s
when boats flew by at 65,
removing the slow and
slow-witted from the crow
gene pool? Or does it mean we lag;
all their adaptation took place
before we pressed a clay-
covered palm to a cave
wall and they evolved perfect timing
to look straight at me—right
through the lens and into
the retina—pick up
and fly off just in time, before
I think, "Jeez, I might hit this one,"
making me so nervous
I swerve, putting myself
and the elderly woman in
the SUV behind me at
risk of serious
injury or worse?

BITTER DECEMBER

I told my San Antonio partners
about the night Ottawa was so cold
the mercury crystallized in the bulb
and we measured temperature in degrees
below zero Kelvin. None of them laughed.
I explained to my Bangalore supplier
that the river ice had frozen so thick
I would have needed chainsaw and augur
to cut through it for pike. The baffled tact
of his reply charmed and disappointed me.
I shared the news with our Costa Rican
bartender: Ottawa was the coldest
city on earth, more frigid than the surface
of Mars where rovers sampled the red sand
for water. He was unmoved by appeals
to the mysteries of other planets.
But you understood because you were there,
walking the dog in the park at midnight,
the nylon leash frozen hockey-stick-stiff,
your eyelashes tinselled with minuscule
icicles, earlobes bleaching with frostbite,
fingertips numb in the buckskin mittens
we snagged at the aboriginal fair,
heartbeat and simmering blood exchanging
your body heat with the world—not because
it was your wish to donate your energy
to the arctic atmosphere framing the stars,
but because we're all subject to the law.

CONSTRUCTING AN ADDITION ON THE OLD HOUSE

1

Would you look at that overcast sky?
Without the sun, the grey, amorphous clouds
buckle like an abandoned farmhouse ceiling,
yawing and sagged, barely clearing six feet,
houseflies suspended in cobwebs for years.
It reminds me—we have
a massive renovation underway.
They say the rubble foundation, shored up
with badly poured concrete three decades ago,
hasn't supported a pound of house for years,
eroded by moisture and rotting posts
of the old balloon frame. I've lived five years
in a dwelling propped up by half-inch-thick
stucco walls. Explains the cracks
I noticed when I bought the place. Good thing
Danica hibernates in the basement;
teens have keen instincts for self-preservation.

2

Gravity isn't an impressive force.
The bats avoid it when they leave the cave
by merely flapping their hands. Look it up.
The parasailing tourists in Grand Cayman
defy it by barely moving a muscle—
Jetskis do all the work, hauling the sails
fifty feet above Caribbean waves.
A blade of grass sprouts straight through the topsoil
and bears the weight of its thousand-seed pod.
Even the atmosphere's not held in place:
every minute, my weight in hydrogen
reaches escape velocity and wanders
with the solar wake beyond the planets.
A year-old baby stands up to gravity.
I feel as light of foot as Karen Kain.
I won't even break a sweat in step class.

3

Hang on a sec, my
mother's on the phone.

4

So it's not gravity but time that moves
the planets in their eccentric orbits,
inflames the knuckles in my mother's hands,
makes porous her bones and erodes her hips.
Arthritis makes it tough for her to smoke.
And her tumour encroaches invisibly,
upward and inward, colonizing vital organs.

5

I think Martin Heidegger got the title
wrong for *Being and Time*. Being in time—
no other way to be. For all the ink
of ontologies since Parmenides,
anguish resists incarnation in words;
it dwells in the skin, the nerves, the neurons.
That thought brings my mother no consolation.
She resents every minute she endures
her aching joints with a bad prescription.

6

Without time—daubing the back of my hand
with sepia calligraphy, each year
marking me with another final point—
Gwen, we wouldn't long for the rhythm of sex.
I couldn't hear you sing or watch you breathe.
My membership in Aeroplan will end
with enough miles for one trip to the moon.
Book my ashes on a rocket there, sweetheart,
though the moon's too light to hold them.

ACCIDENTAL VEGAN

My fridge had more food than I needed.
Jane, I asked you to come to my house and cook with me:
onions, garlic, long beans, fish—no fish!

It was never about the cooking—
you knew that—
it was our way of putting our lips on the same dish.

In the rain, face to face
at the market, we huddled by the fish tank,
watching the slow, sad carp,
gills pulsing, mouth opening, eyes wet, of course.

THE SALINE DIMINISHMENTS

You can barely discern the words—
you misplaced your reading glasses
on the bus. Your contact lenses dried
on your eyes. You slept overnight
at a friend's and brought no saline.
When you remember your daughter,
her tininess—she fit like a chemical

bible on your lap when she was born—
you hold her in the meniscus of herself,
all surface tension at rest until the tube
in the centrifuge of all her days
clarifies her substance and your eyes
recant the belief that you could grasp her.

The undersea barrel of us fills up
with a little brine. Ask any old cooper
who's laid a cask on the seabed: nothing
accelerates the aging of a fine distillation
like saltwater and high pressure.

We've all had extravagant ideas. The worst
must have been the mandrill pianist at the zoo—
never was music more violent.
Keys flew. And yet, the baby danced.

Arizona storms settle scores about the weather;
one grain in a haboob can scratch your cornea.
Dust falls over the ocean too, as I recall.

We subsist on misconceptions,
dust mites on a carpet in the sun.

You can’t return to dust you’ve never left.

HAD A THOUGHT AND LOST IT

There was something we'd been trying to say
for ages. Autumn afternoons, we gathered
at Cousineau's for a pitcher, relaxed the larynx
with Laurentide Ale and let our tongues wag.

It seemed essential to be always only
on the verge of saying anything, as if
we could enlarge what we had to say
by nudging our thoughts beyond our words.

One of us ruined everything, saying—
he must have read it from his notebook—
"The gulf between what we say and what we
want to say must be as wide as the sea,

and, like it, rising." Even Brian knew
he had said too much. Woody, the bartender,
made hollow sounds with his tongue and rattled
Brian's noggin as if it were an empty box.

BIOGRAPHY OF PARENTS

A whistle stuck in your throat.

You recall looking up from the bottom
of a well. How did you get there?

Stuck in your room with a vomiting dog.

Face down in the tub.

Stuck in a Mercury Comet
waiting for them all day.

Stuck in the snow
driving to their funeral.
Will they never relent?

OUTSOURCED MEMORY

I have memory in the trunk,
sticks of it, some defective,

some obsolete. A blue
overcoat, my mother's, covers

memory that might be recovered
if paired with other memory

of the same class. An oil can leaked,
making much of the memory

sticky, tar-smelling, and useless.
Families in vast slums will break

this memory down for rare earth
metals at pennies to the pound.

MARATHON WATER STATION, 24 MILE WAYPOINT

A woman of Ethiopia outpaces
super-fit triathletes who have no thirst to quench.

The blue medical sponges taped to their bodies—
do they absorb sweat and retain it to cool down?

He couldn't be faster: he'd outrun antelope
over this distance but he snags a cup to splash.

A woman announces her pregnancy, not with
a bump, but a placard: I'm Running with Baby.

Batman in full gear: the caped crusader boots it.
Water bottles must be hidden in his Batsuit.

Filling the cups when there's an absence of runners,
water runs along the stone edge of the pavement.

The more slowly a body moves, the more deeply
grateful the voice giving thanks for a few drops.

The barefoot patter of this composed soul: breathing
easy, he snatches a dropless cup from my palm.

I fumble a cup a strong runner reaches for—
he grabs another, looks back at me, smiles, and shrugs.

A pause between packs—there's talk of terror and laws
to forestall it, five hundred yards from Parliament.

The bib pinned to the jersey makes some runners bleed
by the twenty-fourth mile—a thin line of red stain.

Japanese runner, Hinomaru on her shirt,
pumps her knees, rising sun barely damp on her back.

The elderly woman's grey ponytail sways, bobs
on her back, gives rhythm to her satisfied smile.

Kinesio tape on her left knee, a young girl
lurches stationward, synchronizes hand and cup.

Steady palm, outstretched, thumb down, a pivoting hip
to match the runner's pace and keep the pavement dry.

The art of cup-holding: watch the runner without
beseeching, be as transparent as the water.

The shoulders-over-my-head runner, angular,
slow gait, wide stride, snaps his cup, pours it overhead.

A fuchsia sash wraps spandex sweat pants: this woman
runs both for the cure and with advanced sarcoma.

During gaps between packs, we sweep discarded cups,
fearing cracked wet plastic could slide under a foot.

Naught but leather plies between foot sole and pavement,
beard-sporting banker jogs, walks, gives thanks for his cup.

Elvis Aaron Adidas Presley, mid-arch stride,
high knees, strong hound-dog cadence, plucks a Gatorade.

Old scotch strider, knobbed knees buckle under his kilt;
thick liver-spotted claw stretches out for water.

High hop Tigger, exhausted, soaked, and slumped, his tail
a coiled spring stitched to his suit, stops and fills his flask.

Walk, stalwart matron, you've earned each slow step, pause here,
talk with us, take your time swinging back to the road.

FRIED EGG

Turmeric mound
on a bleached shore off Tamil Nadu.

Sunbeam in cloud,
to be so overturned.

Gold on the snow-capped peak
scaled by muscled horns.

Miner waking at dawn,
lift your face from the desert salt flat.

Pollen pools on the concrete,
fallen boughs on the street.

If only the bronze dome of the bank
could slip a disc and be stuck in traction.

The bees, the bees
drowning in other-than-honey.

The eye of that albino gecko in Peru.
There wasn't a wall it wouldn't climb.

The ochre bric-a-brac brickbat
for the graffiti on the porcelain tile.

Soothing amber nightlight
in the white-walled ward no one visits.

If the shadows in the moonlight
dim our midnight faces

and we forget the gratitude
we owe our ancestors,

there will always be breakfast.

BIOGRAPHY OF THE PRAYING MANTA

My father's feet kicked up Accra beach sand
running for surf. Everyone else had fled
because the manta ray circling the cove
was the length of two lean, tobacco-toned,
rum-hardened men of that time. My father
swan-dived into surf and swam under water
as if he were of the sea—the Nominingue
summer camp boy who woke up to light up,
and hung a lit butt on the shower ledge,
could hold his breath one minute on vacation.
My father swam beside the coral reef
and the manta corkscrewed around him—why?
He'd have had no scent of fish or squid on his
Coppertone skin. Bacardi and Rothman's—
no fish. So prayer may be a formalized
greeting and encounter with the other.
I say this because, that summer, he brought me
a praying mantis in a cardboard box.
I returned the mantis to a blade of grass.

SEPTEMBER SHOWERS

Splashed down by
drops of rain
larger than their
bodies, the midges
fly up,
karaoke notes
for a song
I can't recall.
They want
the ripe berries
hanging
from that tree.

IT'S INTERESTING HOW OUR SOCIETY FUNCTIONS

In terms of well-heeled gents
preserved by multiple stents.

In terms of leopard-print body suits
accessorized by vinyl ankle boots.

In terms of parasitic aphids
gorging on the sap of orchids.

In terms of lawyers with Windsor ties
and toddlers gorged on supersize fries.

In terms of the strategist from Jane's
recommending shoes and fighter planes.

In terms of the stand of lodge-pole pine
and the harvest of old-growth vines.

In terms of the 7 a.m. blur
of the February jogger.

And when I say how fortunate
we are just to be here,
you ask me, "In terms of what?"

DRIVING GARBAGE

Don't tell me this never happened to you.
You're late lugging the garbage to the curb.
The compost truck has driven by. August:
neighbours crack jokes about cracking eggs
on hot patio stones and cooking them
sunny-side up in the noon sun. You heft
the reeking green bin into the trunk of your
Honda Civic and pursue the compost truck
with your trunk lid open, maggots dropping
onto the pavement like a trail of crumbs.
An elderly woman out for a walk
shrieks when her terrier Cindy slurps
the squirming lane-markers from the pavement.
The first thought that enters your head—as starlings
join the feast and Cindy yanks on the leash,
snaking her tongue and yawping at the birds
to lay off her succulent victuals—is this:
thank you, Cindy, for ingesting the last
traces of wasted food I left to rot. Your
agile tongue licks the shame from my face.

BIOGRAPHY OF THE GANGSTER UNCLE

My Montreal Pool Room combat lesson:
"You have a good spear if you have a straight cue.
Here, grab it palms down, thumbs up, and learn to
twist and thrust it in a single motion.

Boom! You've pierced a lung or bruised an organ."
My mother let slip that Gary stowed a few
grand in a jar behind loose bricks in the flue
and emptied a locker full of weapons

in the pond before mechanic cancer
let his bookend brother and sister
cremate his remains in a canvas casket.

"Word gets round, they'll wonder where the cash is,"
a friend warned me. "Don't write about it."
Bring it. I have a cue and a jar of ashes.

FALLEN LEAF

This October-bronzed leaf isn't the tree's tear or a flag of grief for the culled elms on our street. The veins aren't a palimpsest; they contain no message to be read when our conscience brings to mind the generations harvested for floors, steps, walls, shelves, books, and December fires. I said, once,

How beautiful the crimson leaf
that falls among the many;
all we as leaves; how ancient the cycle

of the impetuous sun; how like a leaf
my departing mother.

But look, on the webcam—the Atlantic rainforest is greening now. A hummingbird sips from a red plastic feeder. A wasp lands. An emerald blur swallows the wasp mid-flight.

BACON PRODUCTION ON AN INDUSTRIAL SCALE

After I dreamt of bacon
I doubted the planet would ever recover.

Black pigs stanched in vast sties
from here to California.

Sears Towers of grain on the horizon
funnelled feed to troughs the length of Route 66.

Abattoirs the size of Boeing factories.
I can't bring myself to describe the effluent.

Smoke houses sprawled along the Mississippi
like full-throttle coal-fired power plants

air-conditioning the malls of the world
after 100 days of 100-degree heat.

One hog had the face of Noam Chomsky. He said,
"Your disbelief does not make data false."

Knowing eloquent speech is not
the characteristic note of our time,

I protested, "Of course I believe in data, big data,
all of it," to a sow with her nose in the trough.

SANDBAGGING THE RIVER BEFORE THE FLOOD

A ditch becomes a river when water
falls into it, a thought too simple:
a baby could slide down that thought's bank.
An orchard's worth of apple pollen could
daub with yellow the thought that funnels water
and water tunnels through. They say a river
makes its own luck, digs its heels in, nudges
the rocks aside to amble down. The earth
gives way to let the water by.
                                        Now, I'm not
knocking on your door hoping Jehovah
bends you away from your sinful nature
but a river's a declining depression
in the dirt as long as there's water
to fall into it.
          Take the Saint-Laurent
and all its critters: sturgeon so big they
swallowed a tribe, back before
blackflies ate us alive on our first portage
beyond Hochelaga—Asian carp, alien
boat-leapers, invasive plankton vacuums
leaving slim pickings for larval trout and pike—
zebra muscles, hangers-on to every hull
from old Monsieur Beaudoin's leaky Sabot
to a CSL container vessel
larger than the largest riverside
cathedral—otters making all the kids
light up as if the savage predators
were as cuddly as polyester
stuffies—and think about those catadromous
American eels spawning in the salt
Sargasso Sea, eggs floating in scum,

riding the tide back past Anticosti
to the factory at Montmorency Falls
where minke and beluga swim on their backs
or belly up to the sandbar, and Sonja
Paradis brews Mother's Milk tea.
                                        Now, I'm not
calling you up to sell discount hydro
or ask for your vote, but I've been told
there were no rivers in the Sahara.
Imagine. When it does rain, there must be
abundant veins of water in and between
the dunes, and who can say the sand's not soft
on the water? What water there is may
drain a little deeper underground
to bedrock or clay on its long meander
to the factory at Hawamdia,
or from faucet to kettle to bottle
of formula onto the lips of Ayat,
or into the mouth of the Nile perch
at the mouth of the Nile on its way
to the Mediterranean, Homer's
ocean stream.
                    And I'm not driving around
your neighbourhood, ringing my bell, hoping
to sharpen your kitchen knives or grind
your garden shears, but there were rivers on
Mars, don't care if you don't believe it.
I mean, I don't know if there were
living things. Maybe a Martian breeze picked up
the spores of meteorite microbes
and let them fall upstream in Kasei Valles.
Someone called the moment we're living in—
that one, right there, the one that passed us by—
a bubble in a river, and I thought,

now that's a good keepsake for the tongue.
I'm not going to tell you you're a river;
you know you are—and, no, I don't mean
the little wadis and coulees you let down
daily. I think you have an inkling I'm not
leaning on simple biology (vessel,
capillary, urethra, and duct).
That's all part of the egosystem.
You're going to make your way underground,
and when you do, the rain will make its way
over, under, around, and through you,
no matter how waterproof the casket,
no matter how well-sealed the urn. But that's
a harder turn than I wanted to take
with you. Let someone else tell you the shining line
running from your lower eyelid over
your cheek and down the edge of your nostril
to your lip is a river of a kind. They will.
Who am I to dissuade them?

HORIZONTAL SCENE

My lumpy horizon, how your amplitudes
enrich my experience of the sun.
You swallow the container vessel,
proving the planet round.
You gorge on many
an over-burdened skiff,
proving the planet flat
at the local
level, where the action
happens. Mixing bowl of the sea,
you churn a batter of salt
water
and the tiny flies that
fall in
can't climb out for all their wings
and orange life vests.

CONFLICTED THOUGHTS ON OIL PRESSES PAST AND FUTURE

It's difficult to be saddened by the heat
death of the universe. Phil seems to feel

its imminence—at the Cameo Lounge,
sipping rhubarb Stoli through a sage leaf.

Phil chills his Tahoe's leather seats in August,
heats them up in February wind chill

for the Vaughan-Barrie commute in a truck
the size of a juvenile Ankylosaurus

that breathed abundant oxygen when the sun
was cooler, the planet hotter and sediments

pressed the last eon's Plantae for future oil
like those enterprising Pender Island souls

cultivating Canada's first olive grove,
thriving since the planet's warmed up again.

FEEDING TIME AT THE RESORT

The cook litters the water under the dock
with kitchen sea scum: squid guts, fish bladders,
heads, spines, tails. The sandpiper dives for it;
the man o' war snatches it from the air
before it slaps the surface but a man
snorkelling under the dock explains, later,
when I pass him a Spanish Iguana
at happy hour, "I saw the most amazing thing
when I was snorkelling under the dock.
A fish and bird were fighting for the same food,
one a mirror image of the other.
Both had a face you might have recognized;
you know the face—the face of some fucking
Mexican that hasn't eaten for a week."

BIOGRAPHY OF THE DISCOVERED OWL

Harvesting pumpkins,
rolling them to look for rot,
I found an owl, earth-cool
under the leaf sprawl,

examined it—knowing
nothing of owl gender—
no blood marks, too stiff
to reveal broken limbs,

it seemed yet to be insect-
infiltrated, feathers burnished
with late sunlight, talons
clean, sharp, clear at the tips.

To my mother's horror,
I brought it to my father.
He had the coroner of birds,
by art mysterious to me,

preserve and mount it
on a chainsaw-cut post, posed
prior to ensnaring prey, claws wide,
savage, ravenous; not wise.

GROUND POPPIES

When we have boots on the ground,
spring poppies will be trampled.
Given the facts on the ground, we'll deploy
spring poppies in wicker baskets

to comfort the displaced whose shoes are tattered.
The facts above the ground are historic,
unprecedented: songbirds in the apple boughs,
bees inspecting poppies for nectar,

droning of drones. Facts under the ground concern
all those concerned with public health: the roots
of poppies under so many flowerbeds,
twenty thousand boots in ten thousand plots.

NIGHTMARE

Here are a few facts concerning mares that have foaled under the moon. Their teeth are fortified by iron percolated from the earth by the roots of rough grass. Their wombs are inscribed with horse scriptures, symbols imprinted by fetal hooves.

Steel in the foreleg, granite in the hoof.

Your nightmare of the flood, water rising through the basement floor from no visible source, from an urge, a consequence of action or inaction, to the ceiling before you woke in the dream, underwater, watching the foal swim above you from your soft, moist pillow.

What are you doing with your free time?

Why carry that saddle on your shoulders?

ELEVEN SENTENCES ABOUT NOTHING IN PARTICULAR

No one spoke. I'm not sure anyone
inhaled or exhaled.

The power had gone out because of the storm.

It was midnight. Clouds obscured the moon and stars.
The wind subsided.

It was January; no cricket mating songs
echoed in the urban canyon.

No mosquito wings over my ear
radiated undecryptable signals.

No critters foraged through the frozen compost.

I had witnessed the imperceptible, ephemeral—
a breeze the follicles on your arm barely register

that wouldn't disturb the flight path of a fly,

a transition between stillness and the smallest
motion—until

Fred whoop-whoop-whooped, slammed the rim
of the bottle to his lips, swallowed, and

Albert gagged, vaping noxious distillations
sweetly reeking of cardamom and tar.

Potato! I thought, reflecting on absolute
darkness, not of the vacuum of space

replete with illumination in transit,
but of the cavities in the earth

where light has no business,
where a potato grows an eye.

BIOGRAPHY OF MY FATHER'S LAST BREATH

My father says
no more
audibly
than the January
draught
that faintly
whistled
through the gap
in the bedroom
window
he never replaced,
"Have to go," or,
"You have to go," or,
"Time to go."
I can't make
him out.
Even my mother
lets him go
without
insisting
he repeat himself.

FOUR TRUTHS

Disobedient Civic Truth

If I speak truth to the police, I fear my face may become
a canvas for the irrepressible impressionism of the state;
gravel, tar, and blood may paint a masterpiece of flowers
on my cheek. State photographers will archive images of
my face for safekeeping. My career prospects may grow
tenuous. I fear my father will never forgive the humiliation.
The truth I wanted to speak to the police is simply this: I
am raising this banner to the truth to protest lies, officer.
What is a safe distance from which I can speak this truth
to the police?

False Indelicate Truth

I will speak truth to the poor. If they forgo a meal or two to make their rent, or defer episodes of *Duck Dynasty* until they appear on Netflix, I doubt these gaps in nutrition and cultural communion move the needle on the micro-economy of their threadbare lives. If there are water coolers at their places of employment, the workers may take fewer moments to share conversation, increasing productivity. True, they may sleep more fitfully with fewer cigarettes to console themselves. But their perception of the truth will have no effect on commodity prices.

Truth in Family Matters

Speak truth to our mother. I will not. You must. If I speak truth to her, you know what will happen. Moloch, Baal, Gorgon, and Demogorgon—every demon since the dawn of time—will take lodgings in our house for months or years to come. Not even the oak-panelled den will bring refuge. Please, speak truth to our mother. I'm urging you courteously. She's tender to you. I should have brought her oranges in bed on Christmas morning. What can I trade you for candour?

Parental Truth Refusal

Under no circumstances will I speak truth to my daughter. Are you out of your mind, Doctor? No, that doesn't matter. Not to her. If she knew what my father had done, her grandfather, and what I have done. No—it's impossible. I haven't spoken the hard, unvarnished axe handle of the truth even to you, Doctor. There are too few remaining hours to fill them with the truth. I lack the funds for you to assess the impact of the truth on her. By the time we've inspected the truth for its consequences, it will be too late to make a difference.

BIOGRAPHY OF THE LETTERPRESS FATHER

The day after my father died, I swept
a thousand pounds of scrap—plates, rods, wires,
gears—with an industrial broom three feet wide.
I hurled reams of 90 lb cover stock, rolls
of blank newsprint, corrugated cardboard,
pallets of die-cut printed boxboard packed
but never delivered to a customer who never paid.
I dumped his confession from drawers of lead type
on the concrete floor of the loading dock
and shovelled it into the bin below.
I poured endless canisters of unused ink,
blending indigo, emerald, pink, gold, and black
into this grey biography of his adulterous heart.

LOST CAUSES

Let me summarize your thinking.
Rain didn't cause the crocus to grow.

The sun wasn't responsible for the flood.
Your ice cream didn't melt because of the sun.

The glass didn't break because you placed it on the floor.
The running dog didn't cause the wine stain

on the Persian rug. Your fingers
didn't bleed because you picked up broken glass.

The bent stem of wheat didn't cause the ant
to fall, nor did the wind, for what caused

it? Your hand may have been near, cutting a shaft
to dangle from your teeth, aping a rube

tasting the earth through a blade of grass.
I'll concede the odds of the absurd are never zero.

Turn the key in the ignition; floor it.
Not an inch of Florida beach will disappear.

COMMUNITY ANNOUNCEMENTS

1

I left the shells
on the shrimp
in the pad Thai I made
for your most recent visit—
Patagonian, wild, they were
somewhat less than sweet.
Now all of you complain,
"Why do you leave the shell
on everything: the shrimp,
the peanuts, bright blue
quail eggs, your atrophied
heart, malignant tongue?"

2

I have witnessed
a fatal accident—I am
serious; please listen—what
appalls me is not
the blood on the pavement—
burgundy on the black
tar beside the victim's spilled
grocery bag of fruit and vegetables.
No—I am appalled by
the woman taking
pictures with her cellphone
and my irresistible need
to tell you about it. It is as if
she and I had dipped our hands
in the coagulating blood
and hand-painted graffiti on a stone wall:
The blood of this elderly woman is
ink for our sensitive souls.

3

Will be trundling home
shortly. Look for the man
lying
face down on the street,
dragging himself along
by his chin.

BIOGRAPHY OF CALVING

Imagine your mother in retirement
pulling the eighty-pound carcass of a calf
from the barely dilated uterus
of a baying cow
accompanied by the disharmony
of the herd's bovine keening.

She'd securely stanchion the cow's neck.
She'd tie the calf's hind legs with chains
fetched from the shed. She couldn't yank
on the rusted links
and expect the calf to pop out
like a cork from a bottle of blush.

She'd have to dodge the cow's
withering kicks, the blood
and dung it bathes the calf's
hind hooves in,
and bury the carcass that night
so the mother couldn't smell it.

WEDNESDAY MORNING, 3 AM

Nothing more silencing than audits by proxy, filaments of ink crossing the line.

Nothing more silencing than loss of employment in the cathedral ceilings of the boxmall.

Delusional fear opposes silence—gestures with hands, diaphragm, throat, tongue: minimal coherence fortified by rage.

Nothing more silencing than the derisive laughter of intimate companions you have never met but who have eyes and ears.

Nothing more silencing than decreased taxes on the capital's gains at your expense.

The silencing of excess of white bread was unexpected.

Nothing more silencing than excessive praise from the widest circles, dancing around you while you sob, loving the word, hating the temporary blindness.

Nothing more silencing than twenties, freely bestowed, in your foolish, extravagant twenties and your miserly later years.

That explosives are silencing surprised nobody; after all, damage to the eardrum insists upon it.

Nothing more silencing than the fist—the sight of it flying, the smell of it (cologne, gunmetal) landing.

Nothing more silencing than a barrel (a refinement of the previous sentiment in which the projectile limits the agency of the dispatcher).

Intoxication seldom begins with silence, frequently erupts into deafening slurs, and always ends with silence.

Nothing more silencing than hunger in a world of nauseating abundance.

Nothing more silencing than an old-fashioned weapon put to contemporary use.

The cry of a baby is among the most troubling matters of silencing.

Nothing more silencing than these byzantine institutions and their buildings in which the silenced are habitually misplaced.

Nothing more silencing than the lackey who lawyers up to take shelter from the F5 shit-tornado of the violations revealed upon analysis of records gathered from his violated privacy.

The totalizing silence induced by prescription narcotic painkillers was so complete the entire subject eluded conversation.

~~Nothing more silencing than a fag-hating preacher with thundering vowels and a head-cracking officer with a baton. They have the same face—didn't you see?~~

Nothing more silencing than wireless everything.

Nothing more silencing than the twittering of flightless birds.

Although not immediately effective, nothing more silencing than pepper spray in the hands of a protective force.

Nothing more silencing than silence, as if the voice asking the question were a sea breeze from Peru undetected in the absolute stillness of an arctic morning.

WHITE SWEATER, BLACK DOG

When I found Niko's black wire doodle fur on
the white cashmere sweater you re-gifted to me,
I said, "Writing is impossible, unconscionable,"
opened the BBQ and set all my poetry
on fire—my annotated Coleridge, the tiny Faber
Larkin volumes, even *The North Ship*,
the signed, original Contact Press
Poems for All the Annettes, the Musgrave,
the Atwood, Browning's *Aurora Leigh*—that was a difficult
parting (I sold my copy of *The Ring and the Book*
ages ago and made a slim profit on that fat volume),
the Wallace Stevens, even *Opus Posthumous*,
the Anne Carson (I kept *Economy of the Unlost* because
it had thoughts about banking, a subject closer
to my current temperament), my cherished,
foxed *Mountain Tea* with the red ballpoint pen
inscription "To Brocky, a brother in the mysteries,"
Fagles' Homer, all the Greek and Latin Penguins,
Cohen (of course, I kept the music),
Layton (minus *Waiting for the Messiah*),
Klein, Marlatt, Miron, Mallarmé, Hébert, Villeneuve,
Vigneault, Nelligan, Baudelaire, Apollinaire,
Brodsky, Herbert, Milosz, Rimbaud, Solway,
Szymborska, Zagajewski, Pound, Plath,
Pindar, Pinsky—why not send them off with one
last alliteration? When I heaved the poetical works
of Bowering and mclennan on top of the pile,
I feared the arrival of local bylaw officers,
but, after I heaped on my own books,
scribbled manuscripts and drafts, squirt-squirt,
up rose a magnificent flame more colourful
than I would have imagined, so hot

it seared my eyebrows, so bright
my retina retained the image for days.
We cooked dry-aged steaks on the coals,
ate them rare, and laughed together.
Oh, we ate well, and fed our doodle the fat.

BIOGRAPHY OF MATERNAL VIGILANCE

With her, there was always a "Where do you
think you're going with that,

mister?" The going throttled, the you
curtailed, the that confiscated—

but of the thinking let me say a few words:
it grew devious.

Hash in a hidden pocket of my jeans.
Roxanne under my bed until midnight.

Her rum meticulously diluted.
A kiss on her cheek in her coma.

CABLE NEWS BRIEFING

1

You sob; blood lots
from your only property—
limbs, noggin,
cerebrum,
auditory nerves—
pool in eddies
in your ventricles,
turbulent
song.

2

As a philanthropist, I corral the colonies of black ants in my yard with meticulously crafted miniature barbed-wire fences.

As an anarchist with decades of governance inexperience, I was surprisingly enthused that my uprising lyrics were untrusted.

As a barista on hiatus, may I offer you a thought-free word salad with the emptiness you subscribed to online? Don't you love my small-cap khaki slacks?

3

Theft of your purse—
lip beaded with blood.
Theft of your words—
tongue,
wired for sound,
grounded.

4

As an undertaker, I urge you to think of me as the entrepreneur of happy departures, the purveyor of first resort for your all-inclusive last resort, piña coladas and all.

As the timekeeper for this community rink, I can tell you everything you need to know about eternity.

As corporate librarian, I can attest we do not have a single volume of poetry to lend you. We would prefer you keep your body of work to yourself, covered.

5

Schlep on, traveller;
your destination lies
before you, beside you,
behind you.

Dry your brow.
How freshening the permafrost
bed under these sun-radiating
pavements of cracked stone.

6

As the shepherd of the pasture on the last undeveloped parcel in this ex-urb, I admonish the sheep for its black wool.

BUTTERFLY ON CRUSHED GRAVEL

Butterfly, your wings are mirror
haiku, hand-painted
on fine yellow paper
the breeze has opened
for reading. I can't read them.
You have no soul. No big deal.
Why rest on the hot gravel?
I might have crushed you
or stepped over you
if I had not been looking down.
I have a photograph
of my daughter with butterflies
on her arm and in her hair.
She would laugh if I sent her
an image of you, lost
in the hair on my arm.
Why will you not be moved?
Science explains nothing.

BIOGRAPHY OF MY MOTHER'S ASHES

Here is a selfie with my mother's urn.
And here is a snapshot of her ashes
in the urn. Morbid? Sure. But I've always
wondered what cremated remains look like
before they're scattered. Similar, I'd say,
to weeks of stubbed-out cigarette ashes
from one of her scorched porcelain ashtrays.
And here is a photo of the urn strapped
into the passenger seat of my Honda
on our way to the farm where she must have
lived her most cherished moments: at least she
laughed, slept solo, breathed fresh air, fed cattle,
walked fields, nurtured generations of cats.
And here is a shot of the new owner,
Mme Chevaucher, looking nonplussed but
hospitable—to think she welcomes me
to the house where, at a different moment,
I hid behind this door, creaking the hinges,
dodging a beer thrown at me by McGimpsey.
I took this image while Mme Chevaucher
brewed a pot of fresh coffee. You can see
her bewilderment: arms crossed at her chest,
the corner of one lip curled upward
to say, "I'm not sure I like this idea."
Here, at a distance, Mme Chevaucher waves
as I trudge bushward backward in dress shoes,
making the image blurred and off-kilter.
I took the next selfie with shovel and urn
after I dug a pit in the clearing
near cedar and tamarack, by the pond
we dredged and cleared of bulrushes.
It was always too cattle-shit filthy

to sustain anything but monstrous frogs
that thrived on deerflies the size of your thumb.
My necktie is a bib of earth and ash.
What memorabilia would you have chosen
to inter with the urn? Her bronze cup
commemorating 32 years' service?
The charm bracelet my father lavished on her—
gold repaid in the currency of forbearance?
Even in the aluminum tin, I doubt
her old family photographs would last.
How might future archaeologists compare
Neanderthal burials with this Spartan plot?
Ancient graves saved corpses from scavengers.
No fox-fodder in ash. No worm meal there.
I buried the urn with the lid open.
Maybe she could fertilize a few sprigs.
Here Mme Chevaucher greets my return
with a sympathetic smile. I hadn't
noticed she's missing more than one tooth.
In this one she waves goodbye through the lines
of the rear window. Look, in this last one:
the passenger seat is empty but soiled.

SUBJECT TO QUESTION

All my ideas of beauty are subject to question
and my gratitude is boundless.

The bankers of Chengdu know their places
in the gleaming offices nudging the clouds;

the towers gleam thanks to the Sun—please,
if you trust me in one thing trust me in this—

and the Bentley shines in the car park,
buffed by a hand. When I rejoice at the guitar

stylings of Manuel López, when I adore
your evening closet stride,

when a child sings like an angel—
I imagine celestial music—

when I admire the snowfall in the park,
I voluntarily subscribe to the anxiety

of beauty affirmed by the involuntary
insurrection of muscle
at the base of each follicle of my arms.

PERFECTLY LUCID SQUIRREL

As I was walking up Acacia Avenue
on an overcast afternoon in June,
a cold wind, carried south to us
by the decaying polar vortex,
caught my throat, threatening
my compromised immune system.
It was a wind cold enough for me
to wear three layers of wool and a hoodie.
Let me say the wool underwear
my mother gave me for my birthday
was a welcome comfort. As I strode
up the hill beneath the swaying branches,
a hybridized black-and-grey squirrel,
with black roots and grey tips—or
it may have been black in front and grey behind,
or it may have shifted from one state to another—
crossed my path, and paused on the road
without a question mark in its tail but
with a perfectly vertical exclamation mark.
Now, whether his tail presented itself
in such a declamatory fashion
because it had been severed at the tip
or because it was an evolutionary adaptation
to more readily survive the distracted
local drivers, as if evolution proposed
rather than ask, "Why?" exclaim, "Hear me!"
what the squirrel did next astonished me—

How to put this? The squirrel had
a mind as vast as the universe—you could
see in its eyes miraculously perfect
assertions appear one symbol at a time
in response to silent queries.
Soon two lines of cars drew to a stop.
The drivers were too enchanted by
the squirrel's profound symbolic engagement
to honk their horns; their minds undistracted,
they shut down their cars and smart phones,
and sat on the street around the squirrel.
Neighbours and community leaders
attended the squirrel; each of us asked questions
and received answers in a miracle of
simultaneity. The local coffee shop offered
fair trade java from Ecuador as all of us
continued to interrogate the squirrel.
We received answers we knew immediately to be true
because we could recreate the steps to knowing them—
I know you disbelieve this—
but you will be astonished by the evidence—

No, I can't seem to recall the proof
for the existence of dark matter. I've lost
my notes in these disordered bookshelves.
I remember marking down the symbols.
I'm not sure you can imagine
the pleasure we shared, having the knowledge
of such truth in the way one has
knowledge of the truth of one's hands.
We were liberated from the fear
and distrust inherent in belief.
His assertions were self-proving
in the perfection of their phrasing,
each deduction as ineluctable as a breath.
Now, in the dandelions by the curb,
Max, our neighbour's tom, having
bored of the bumblebee he had been
tormenting in the grass among the scattered
petals of a poppy, entered that predatory
feline pose, vectoring his paws
in the direction of the squirrel.
It was the first moment I had broken off
the squirrel's gaze. I noticed I was unable
to speak or move. I couldn't
wave my arms to break the squirrel from its
dozens of simultaneous conversations.
I tried to reengage with the squirrel,
attempting, rather than a question,
an imperative: "Save yourself, so that we
may forever know what we know without fear!"
How the squirrel responded
in the next few moments
will amaze you—

The squirrel intimated to me
that he was the dolphin of the maple branches,
and the cat the orca of the urban grass,
as entitled to his prey as the ocean bed
to the currents of water that run over it,
and I—I was the
sea cucumber of the plywood box
to which I anchored my small
but firmly gripping feet.

FAREWELL WITH A GUITAR

He drank at noon from a bottle
he would empty by sunset.

Let him strum a chord here,
in the living room, to close the evening.

Let the gravel in his throat,
more percussive than lyrical,

drone, out of tune and out of time,
his misremembering of an old folk song.

COMA

When you wake from your coma, let there be,
if not peace in the world, peace in the ward;
if not among all of us and our masters,
then peace among the nursing staff on the floor
at that moment, peace between orderlies
and nurses, between nurses and physicians,
peace, even, among emergency room
patients, paramedics and police, peace
between hospital administrators, who
smile broadly, porcelain caps sparkling.
Let there be babies nearby—I don't care
if they cry—I would rather the babies
wail you out of your coma than angels
bugle your gleaming corpse to Paradise.

BIOGRAPHY OF MISTAKEN IDENTITIES

I was mistaken for Steve Martin at a bar in Montreal.
I was mistaken for someone Richard Simmons could love
by Richard Simmons on a flight to Los Angeles.
I was mistaken for Olympian Ken Read
but I've never needed skis to hurtle downhill.
I was mistaken for a gay man at Swizzles
and played it to my advantage at the slam.
I was such a flirt! Were they mistaken?
I am told I could be mistaken for Henry Rollins.
Soon my dog will mistake me for an old hound
on the porch, bark in my face, and tear my ears.
I hope to be mistaken for soil by seedling pines.

ACKNOWLEDGEMENTS

Thanks to the journals and small presses that published some of these poems: *Arc, Inwords, Matrix, MTLS, Ottawater, Prism International, The Puritan,* David Stymeist's Textualis Press (*Where Did You See It Last?*) and rob mclennan's above/ground press (*Declassified Nuclear Test Films*).

Roland Prevost, Pearl Pirie, and Janice Tokar were inspiring and generous collaborators. The Ottawa writing community is a background collaborator—I feel fortunate to live in a city with plentiful, energetic literary venues, small press publishers, and zines. Thanks to rob mclennan and Christine McNair for their tireless efforts with above/ground press and Chaudiere Books. The Factory Reading Series, curated by rob, brings poets together from across North America. Sean Wilson and Kira Harris at the Ottawa International Writers Festival have generously invited me to participate as guest and host. VerseFest is a unique international festival of poetry that has become indispensable: thank you to Vivian Vavassis, Avonlea Fotheringham, Monty Reid, David O'Meara, David Stymeist, and, of course, Rod Pederson. I'd also like to thank Jennifer Pederson for starting the gritty, innovative Sawdust reading series. I've test-driven almost every poem in this book at one of these venues.

I'm grateful to the Canada Council for the Arts for a generous grant at an important time.

Stuart Ross, you are the "details follow" of this book's existence.

My daughter, Danica Brockwell, makes poetry happen every day with her curiosity and sense of justice.

Gwendolyn Guth—I'm reticent to communicate my gratitude for your irrepressible, joyful nature here; you are muse, first collaborator, and final editor.

Stephen Brockwell cut his writing teeth in the '80s in Montreal, appearing on French and English CBC Radio and in the anthologies *Cross/cut: Contemporary English Quebec Poetry* and *The Insecurity of Art* (both Véhicule Press, 1982). George Woodcock described Brockwell's first book, *The Wire in Fences*, as having an "extraordinary range of empathies and perceptions." Harold Bloom wrote that Brockwell's second book, *Cometology*, "held rare and authentic promise." *Fruitfly Geographic* won the Archibald Lampman Award for best book of poetry in Ottawa in 2005. Brockwell currently operates a small IT consulting company from the seventh floor of the Chateau Laurier and lives in a house perpetually under construction.

OTHER BOOKS FROM MANSFIELD PRESS

Poetry

Leanne Averbach, *Fever*
Tara Azzopardi, *Last Stop, Lonesome Town*
Nelson Ball, *In This Thin Rain*
Nelson Ball, *Some Mornings*
Gary Barwin, *Moon Baboon Canoe*
George Bowering, *Teeth: Poems 2006–2011*
Stephen Brockwell, *Complete Surprising Fragments of Improbable Books*
Stephen Brockwell & Stuart Ross, eds., *Rogue Stimulus: The Stephen Harper Holiday Anthology for a Prorogued Parliament*
Diana Fitzgerald Bryden, *Learning Russian*
Alice Burdick, *Book of Short Sentences*
Alice Burdick, *Flutter*
Alice Burdick, *Holler*
Sarah Burgoyne, *Saint Twin*
Jason Camlot, *What The World Said*
Margaret Christakos, *wipe.under.a.love*
Pino Coluccio, *First Comes Love*
Marie-Ève Comtois, *My Planet of Kites*
Dani Couture, *YAW*
Gary Michael Dault, *The Milk of Birds*
Frank Davey, *Poems Suitable to Current Material Conditions*
Pier Giorgio Di Cicco, *The Dark Time of Angels*
Pier Giorgio Di Cicco, *Dead Men of the Fifties*
Pier Giorgio Di Cicco, *The Honeymoon Wilderness*
Pier Giorgio Di Cicco, *Living in Paradise*
Pier Giorgio Di Cicco, *My Life, Without Me*
Pier Giorgio Di Cicco, *Early Works*
Pier Giorgio Di Cicco, *The Visible World*
Salvatore Difalco, *What Happens at Canals*
Christopher Doda, *Aesthetics Lesson*
Christopher Doda, *Among Ruins*
Glen Downie, *Monkey Soap*
Rishma Dunlop, *The Body of My Garden*
Rishma Dunlop, *Lover Through Departure: New and Selected Poems*
Rishma Dunlop, *Metropolis*
Rishma Dunlop & Priscila Uppal, eds., *Red Silk: An Anthology of South Asian Women Poets*
Ollivier Dyens, *The Profane Earth*
Laura Farina, *Some Talk of Being Human*
Jaime Forsythe, *Sympathy Loophole*
Carole Glasser Langille, *Late in a Slow Time*
Eva HD, *Rotten Perfect Mouth*
Eva HD, *Wolverine States*
Suzanne Hancock, *Another Name for Bridge*
Jason Heroux, *Emergency Hallelujah*
Jason Heroux, *Hard Work Cheering Up Sad Machines*
Jason Heroux, *Memoirs of an Alias*
Jason Heroux, *Natural Capital*
John B. Lee, *In the Terrible Weather of Guns*
Jeanette Lynes, *The Aging Cheerleader's Alphabet*
David W. McFadden, *Abnormal Brain Sonnets*
David W. McFadden, *Be Calm, Honey*
David W. McFadden, *Shouting Your Name Down the Well: Tankas and Haiku*
David W. McFadden, *What's the Score?*
Kathryn Mockler, *The Purpose Pitch*
Leigh Nash, *Goodbye, Ukulele*
Lillian Necakov, *The Bone Broker*
Lillian Necakov, *Hooligans*
Peter Norman, *At the Gates of the Theme Park*
Peter Norman, *Water Damage*
Natasha Nuhanovic, *Stray Dog Embassy*
Catherine Owen & Joe Rosenblatt, *Dog*
Corrado Paina, *The Alphabet of the Traveler*
Corrado Paina, *Cinematic Taxi*
Corrado Paina, *The Dowry of Education*
Corrado Paina, *Hoarse Legend*
Corrado Paina, *Souls in Plain Clothes*
Nick Papaxanthos, *Love Me Tender*
Stuart Ross et al., *Our Days in Vaudeville*
Matt Santateresa, *A Beggar's Loom*
Matt Santateresa, *Icarus Redux*
Ann Shin, *The Last Thing Standing*
Jim Smith, *Back Off, Assassin! New and Selected Poems*
Jim Smith, *Happy Birthday, Nicanor Parra*
Robert Earl Stewart, *Campfire Radio Rhapsody*
Robert Earl Stewart, *Something Burned on the Southern Border*
Meaghan Strimas, *Yes or Nope*
Carey Toane, *The Crystal Palace*
Aaron Tucker, *Punchlines*
Priscila Uppal, *Sabotage*
Priscila Uppal, *Summer Sport: Poems*
Priscila Uppal, *Winter Sport: Poems*
Steve Venright, *Floors of Enduring Beauty*
Brian Wickers, *Stations of the Lost*

Fiction

Marianne Apostolides, *The Lucky Child*
Sarah Dearing, *The Art of Sufficient Conclusions*
Denis De Klerck, ed., *Particle & Wave: A Mansfield Omnibus of Electro-Magnetic Fiction*
Salvatore Difalco, *Mean Season*
Paula Eisenstein, *Flip Turn*
Sara Heinonen, *Dear Leaves, I Miss You All*
Christine Miscione, *Carafola*
Marko Sijan, *Mongrel*
Tom Walmsley, *Dog Eat Rat*
Corinne Wasilewski, *Live from the Underground*

Non-Fiction

George Bowering, *How I Wrote Certain of My Books*
Denis De Klerck & Corrado Paina, eds., *College Street–Little Italy: Toronto's Renaissance Strip*
Pier Giorgio Di Cicco, *Municipal Mind: Manifestos for the Creative City*
Amy Lavender Harris, *Imagining Toronto*
David W. McFadden, *Mother Died Last Summer*
Deborah Verginella, ed., *Bon Appetito Toronto!*

For more information on these titles, and to order books, please visit www.mansfieldpress.net